MW00908899

Dedication

Presented to:

On the Occasion of:

By:

Date:

Songs of Praise

Selection and arrangement © Scandinavia Publishing House 2000.
Scripture quotations are from the Holy Bible, New International Version.
© 2000, International Bible Society.
A co-production from Scandinavia Publishing House,
Drejervej 11-21, DK-2400 Copenhagen NV, Denmark.
Tel.: (+45) 35 31 03 30   Fax.: (+45) 35 31 03 34
Homepage: www.scanpublishing.dk   E-mail: jvo@scanpublishing.dk

Quotations and paintings selected by Scandinavia Publishing House.
Compiled by Tomas Vium Olesen.
Design by Pete Burke.
Printed in Malaysia
ISBN 87-7247-250-2

Songs *of* Praise

- meditating on the Word of God

SCANDINAVIA PUBLISHING HOUSE

Foreword

Who can imagine a room with a marvelous view, but no window? The room might be positioned just right, but there could be no way of knowing its attractive position. It could just as well have been located somewhere else, in a basement or in a prison, and no one would notice the difference from the inside. There would be no possibility of enjoying the beautiful surroundings or allowing the fresh air and sunshine to fill the room, or to even know about it. How sad!

Maybe someone has lived there for a long time, and in all the many times he has trudged up and down the stairs, forgotten the magnificent view just outside that room. Maybe in his wildest dreams he can no longer imagine what he is missing, or maybe he is simply afraid to let the light fill the room. Maybe he doesn't want to see its contents. The person in the room may have many reasons, but one thing is for sure, he has missed out on something of great worth in his life.

The apostle John begins his Gospel by describing God's Word, Jesus Christ, as the Light of men. John was born in a dark time, when Israel, God's chosen people, was an occupied nation. Later on in the same Gospel, he quotes Jesus saying, "I am the Light of the world. Whoever follows Me will never walk in darkness, but will have the Light of life." (John 8:12)

It was the intention of God to have fellowship with man, but man turned his back on God, trying to find his own way. From this position God tried to awaken man by sending His Word, Jesus Christ, His own Son. But because we have turned our backs on God, we cannot see this great Light. Instead we only see our own sinful shadow. We need to be converted.

The prayer that accompanies this book is that it will make a joyful sound in your ear, that it would help you to live in the conversion of Christ, and that it would shed light on your path as you move forward. The songs and psalms of the Bible are tremendously powerful in expressing a wide variety of emotions. Their starting point is always the inner life of man. And rather than abandoning man to himself, they bring him right to the heart of God. Let this book bring you to the very heart of God.

Vilhelm Hammershøi, "Dust Motes dancing in Sunlight"

For with you is the fountain of life; in your light we see light.

Psalm 36:9

Contents

"Star-studded Firmament"

Adoration

I will praise you, O LORD, with all my heart;
before the "gods" I will sing your praise.
I will bow down towards your holy temple
and will praise your name
for your love and your faithfulness,
for you have exalted above all things
your name and your word.
When I called, you answered me;
you made me bold and stout-hearted.
May all the kings of the earth praise you, O LORD,
when they hear the words of your mouth.
May they sing of the ways of the LORD,
for the glory of the LORD is great.
Though the LORD is on high, he looks upon the lowly,
but the proud he knows from afar.
Though I walk in the midst of trouble,
you preserve my life;
you stretch out your hand against the anger of my foes,
with your right hand you save me.
The LORD will fulfil his purpose for me;
your love, O LORD, endures for ever—
do not abandon the works of your hands.

Psalm 138:1-8

Six days before the Passover, Jesus arrived at Bethany, where Lazarus lived, whom Jesus had raised from the dead. Here a dinner was given in Jesus' honour. Martha served, while Lazarus was among those reclining at the table with him. Then Mary took about a pint of pure nard, an expensive perfume; she poured it on Jesus' feet and wiped his feet with her hair. And the house was filled with the fragrance of the perfume.

But one of his disciples, Judas Iscariot, who was later to betray him, objected, "Why wasn't this perfume sold and the money given to the poor? It was worth a year's wages." He did not say this because he cared about the poor but because he was a thief; as keeper of the money bag, he used to help himself to what was put into it.

"Leave her alone," Jesus replied. "It was intended that she should save this perfume for the day of my burial. You will always have the poor among you, but you will not always have me."

John 12:1-8

Love

I love you, O LORD, my strength.
The LORD is my rock, my fortress and my deliverer;
my God is my rock, in whom I take refuge.
He is my shield and the horn of my salvation, my stronghold.
I call to the LORD, who is worthy of praise,
and I am saved from my enemies.
The cords of death entangled me;
the torrents of destruction overwhelmed me.
The cords of the grave coiled around me;
the snares of death confronted me.
In my distress I called to the LORD;
I cried to my God for help.
From his temple he heard my voice;
my cry came before him, into his ears.
He reached down from on high and took hold of me;
he drew me out of deep waters.
He rescued me from my powerful enemy,
from my foes, who were too strong for me.
They confronted me in the day of my disaster,
but the LORD was my support.
He brought me out into a spacious place;
he rescued me because he delighted in me.

Psalm 18:1-6, 16-19

John Samuel Raven, "Near Dunkeld"

Where can I go from your Spirit?
Where can I flee from your presence?
If I go up to the heavens, you are there;
if I make my bed in the depths, you are there.
If I rise on the wings of the dawn,
if I settle on the far side of the sea,
even there your hand will guide me,
your right hand will hold me fast.
If I say, "Surely the darkness will hide me
and the light become night around me,"
even the darkness will not be dark to you;
the night will shine like the day,
for darkness is as light to you.
For you created my inmost being;
you knit me together in my mother's womb.
I praise you because I am fearfully and wonderfully made;
your works are wonderful,
I know that full well.
My frame was not hidden from you
when I was made in the secret place.
When I was woven together in the depths of the earth,
your eyes saw my unformed body.
All the days ordained for me
were written in your book before one of them came to be.

Psalm 139:7-16

Surrender

Large crowds were travelling with Jesus, and turning to them he said: "If anyone comes to me and does not hate his father and mother, his wife and children, his brothers and sisters - yes, even his own life - he cannot be my disciple. And anyone who does not carry his cross and follow me cannot be my disciple.

"Suppose one of you wants to build a tower. Will he not first sit down and estimate the cost to see if he has enough money to complete it? For if he lays the foundation and is not able to finish it, everyone who sees it will ridicule him, saying, 'This fellow began to build and was not able to finish.'

"Or suppose a king is about to go to war against another king. Will he not first sit down and consider whether he is able with ten thousand men to oppose the one coming against him with twenty thousand? If he is not able, he will send a delegation while the other is still a long way off and will ask for terms of peace. In the same way, any of you who does not give up everything he has cannot be my disciple.

"Salt is good, but if it loses its saltiness, how can it be made salty again? It is fit neither for the soil nor for the manure heap; it is thrown out.

"He who has ears to hear, let him hear."

Luke 14:25-35

Christian Købke, "Study of Surf near Marina Piccola, Capri"

I will praise you, O LORD.
Although you were angry with me,
your anger has turned away
and you have comforted me.
Surely God is my salvation;
I will trust and not be afraid.
The LORD, the LORD, is my strength and my song;
he has become my salvation.
With joy you will draw water
from the wells of salvation.
In that day you will say:
Give thanks to the LORD, call on his name;
make known among the nations what he has done,
and proclaim that his name is exalted.
Sing to the LORD, for he has done glorious things;
let this be known to all the world.
Shout aloud and sing for joy, people of Zion,
for great is the Holy One of Israel among you.

Isaiah 12:1-6

Edification

Praise the LORD, O my soul,
and forget not all his benefits—
who forgives all your sins
and heals all your diseases,
who redeems your life from the pit
and crowns you with love and compassion,
who satisfies your desires with good things
so that your youth is renewed like the eagle's.
The LORD works righteousness
and justice for all the oppressed.
He made known his ways to Moses,
his deeds to the people of Israel:
The LORD is compassionate and gracious,
slow to anger, abounding in love.
He will not always accuse,
nor will he harbour his anger for ever;
he does not treat us as our sins deserve
or repay us according to our iniquities.
For as high as the heavens are above the earth,
so great is his love for those who fear him;
as far as the east is from the west,
so far has he removed our transgressions from us.

Psalm 103:2-12

Comfort, comfort my people,
says your God.
Speak tenderly to Jerusalem,
and proclaim to her
that her hard service has been completed,
that her sin has been paid for,
that she has received from the LORD's hand
double for all her sins.
A voice of one calling:
"In the desert prepare
the way for the LORD;
make straight in the wilderness
a highway for our God.
Every valley shall be raised up,
every mountain and hill made low;
the rough ground shall become level,
the rugged places a plain.
And the glory of the LORD will be revealed,
and all mankind together will see it.
For the mouth of the LORD has spoken."

Isaiah 40:1-5

Transformation

For you were once darkness, but now you are light in the Lord.
Live as children of light (for the fruit of the light consists in all
goodness, righteousness and truth) and find out what pleases the Lord. Have
nothing to do with the fruitless deeds of darkness, but rather
expose them. For it is shameful even to mention what the disobedient
do in secret. But everything exposed by the light becomes visible, for it is light
that makes everything visible. This is why it is said:

"Wake up, O sleeper,
rise from the dead,
and Christ will shine on you."

Be very careful, then, how you live—not as unwise but as wise, making the
most of every opportunity, because the days are evil.
Therefore do not be foolish, but understand what the Lord's will is. Do not get
drunk on wine, which leads to debauchery. Instead, be filled with the Spirit.
Speak to one another with psalms, hymns and spiritual songs. Sing and make
music in your heart to the Lord, always giving thanks to God the Father for
everything, in the name of our Lord Jesus Christ.

Ephesians 5:8-20

The Form of Praise

Contemplation

Worship

Celebration

Proclamation

Thanksgiving

"The three Magi"

Contemplation

My soul finds rest in God alone;
my salvation comes from him.
He alone is my rock and my salvation;
he is my fortress, I shall never be shaken.
How long will you assault a man?
Would all of you throw him down—
this leaning wall, this tottering fence?
They fully intend to topple him
from his lofty place;
they take delight in lies.
With their mouths they bless,
but in their hearts they curse. Selah
Find rest, O my soul, in God alone;
my hope comes from him.
He alone is my rock and my salvation;
he is my fortress, I shall not be shaken.
My salvation and my honour depend on God;
he is my mighty rock, my refuge.
Trust in him at all times, O people;
pour out your hearts to him,
for God is our refuge. Selah

Psalm 62:1-8

Edouard Manet, "Moonlight on Boulogne Harbour"

Worship

Praise the LORD.
Praise the LORD from the heavens,
praise him in the heights above.
Praise him, all his angels,
praise him, all his heavenly hosts.
Praise him, sun and moon,
praise him, all you shining stars.
Praise him, you highest heavens
and you waters above the skies.
Let them praise the name of the LORD,
for he commanded and they were created.
He set them in place for ever and ever;
he gave a decree that will never pass away.
Praise the LORD from the earth,
you great sea creatures and all ocean depths,
lightning and hail, snow and clouds,
stormy winds that do his bidding,
you mountains and all hills,
fruit trees and all cedars,
wild animals and all cattle,
small creatures and flying birds,
kings of the earth and all nations,
you princes and all rulers on earth,
young men and maidens, old men and children.

Psalm 148:1-12

Then I saw a Lamb, looking as if it had been slain, standing in the centre of the throne, encircled by the four living creatures and the elders. He had seven horns and seven eyes, which are the seven spirits of God sent out into all the earth. He came and took the scroll from the right hand of him who sat on the throne. And when he had taken it, the four living creatures and the twenty-four elders fell down before the Lamb. Each one had a harp and they were holding golden bowls full of incense, which are the prayers of the saints. And they sang a new song:

"You are worthy to take the scroll
and to open its seals,
because you were slain,
and with your blood you purchased men for God
from every tribe and language and people and nation.
You have made them to be a kingdom and priests to serve our God,
and they will reign on the earth."

Revelation 5:6-10

Celebration

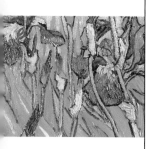

Praise the LORD.
Praise the LORD, O my soul.
I will praise the LORD all my life;
I will sing praise to my God as long as I live.
Do not put your trust in princes,
in mortal men, who cannot save.
When their spirit departs, they return to the ground;
on that very day their plans come to nothing.
Blessed is he whose help is the God of Jacob,
whose hope is in the LORD his God,
the Maker of heaven and earth,
the sea, and everything in them—
the LORD, who remains faithful for ever.
He upholds the cause of the oppressed
and gives food to the hungry.
The LORD sets prisoners free,
the LORD gives sight to the blind,
the LORD lifts up those who are bowed down,
the LORD loves the righteous.
The LORD watches over the alien
and sustains the fatherless and the widow,
but he frustrates the ways of the wicked.
The LORD reigns for ever,
your God, O Zion, for all generations. Praise the LORD.

Psalm 146:1-10

As they approached Jerusalem and came to Bethphage on the Mount of Olives, Jesus sent two disciples, saying to them, "Go to the village ahead of you, and at once you will find a donkey tied there, with her colt by her. Untie them and bring them to me. If anyone says anything to you, tell him that the Lord needs them, and he will send them right away."

This took place to fulfil what was spoken through the prophet:

"Say to the Daughter of Zion,

'See, your king comes to you,

gentle and riding on a donkey,

on a colt, the foal of a donkey.' "

The disciples went and did as Jesus had instructed them. They brought the donkey and the colt, placed their cloaks on them, and Jesus sat on them. A very large crowd spread their cloaks on the road, while others cut branches from the trees and spread them on the road. The crowds that went ahead of him and those that followed shouted,

"Hosanna to the Son of David!"

"Blessed is he who comes in the name of the Lord!"

"Hosanna in the highest!"

When Jesus entered Jerusalem, the whole city was stirred and asked, "Who is this?"

The crowds answered, "This is Jesus, the prophet from Nazareth in Galilee."

Matthew 21:1-11

Proclamation

The Spirit of the Sovereign LORD is on me,
because the LORD has anointed me
to preach good news to the poor.
He has sent me to bind up the broken-hearted,
to proclaim freedom for the captives
and release from darkness for the prisoners,
to proclaim the year of the LORD's favour
and the day of vengeance of our God,
to comfort all who mourn,
and provide for those who grieve in Zion—
to bestow on them a crown of beauty
instead of ashes,
the oil of gladness
instead of mourning,
and a garment of praise
instead of a spirit of despair.
They will be called oaks of righteousness,
a planting of the LORD
for the display of his splendour.
They will rebuild the ancient ruins
and restore the places long devastated;
they will renew the ruined cities
that have been devastated for generations.

Isaiah 61:1-4

Vincent van Gogh, "Irises"

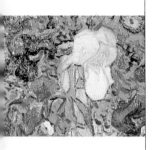

Blessed are the poor in spirit,
for theirs is the kingdom of heaven.
Blessed are those who mourn,
for they will be comforted.
Blessed are the meek,
for they will inherit the earth.
Blessed are those who hunger and thirst for righteousness,
for they will be filled.
Blessed are the merciful,
for they will be shown mercy.
Blessed are the pure in heart,
for they will see God.
Blessed are the peacemakers,
for they will be called sons of God.
Blessed are those who are persecuted because of righteousness,
for theirs is the kingdom of heaven.
Blessed are you when people insult you, persecute you and
falsely say all kinds of evil against you because of me. Rejoice
and be glad, because great is your reward in heaven, for in the
same way they persecuted the prophets who were before you.

Matthew 5:3-12

Thanksgiving

Praise the LORD.
How good it is to sing praises to our God,
how pleasant and fitting to praise him!
The LORD builds up Jerusalem;
he gathers the exiles of Israel.
He heals the broken-hearted
and binds up their wounds.
He determines the number of the stars
and calls them each by name.
Great is our Lord and mighty in power;
his understanding has no limit.
The LORD sustains the humble
but casts the wicked to the ground.
Sing to the LORD with thanksgiving;
make music to our God on the harp.
He covers the sky with clouds;
he supplies the earth with rain
and makes grass grow on the hills.
He provides food for the cattle
and for the young ravens when they call.
His pleasure is not in the strength of the horse,
nor his delight in the legs of a man;
the LORD delights in those who fear him,
who put their hope in his unfailing love.

Psalm 147:1-11

One day Peter and John were going up to the temple at the time of prayer—at three in the afternoon. Now a man crippled from birth was being carried to the temple gate called Beautiful, where he was put every day to beg from those going into the temple courts. When he saw Peter and John about to enter, he asked them for money. Peter looked straight at him, as did John. Then Peter said, "Look at us!" So the man gave them his attention, expecting to get something from them.

Then Peter said, "Silver or gold I do not have, but what I have I give you. In the name of Jesus Christ of Nazareth, walk." Taking him by the right hand, he helped him up, and instantly the man's feet and ankles became strong. He jumped to his feet and began to walk. Then he went with them into the temple courts, walking and jumping, and praising God. When all the people saw him walking and praising God, they recognised him as the same man who used to sit begging at the temple gate called Beautiful, and they were filled with wonder and amazement at what had happened to him.

Acts 3:1-10

The School of Praise

Prayer

Confession

Preservation

Renewal

Faithfulness

"St. Peter and St. Andrew leave the Nets
to follow Christ"

Prayer

Hear, O LORD, my righteous plea;
listen to my cry.
Give ear to my prayer—
it does not rise from deceitful lips.
May my vindication come from you;
may your eyes see what is right.
Though you probe my heart and examine me at night,
though you test me, you will find nothing;
I have resolved that my mouth will not sin.
As for the deeds of men—
by the word of your lips
I have kept myself
from the ways of the violent.
My steps have held to your paths;
my feet have not slipped.
I call on you, O God, for you will answer me;
give ear to me and hear my prayer.
Show the wonder of your great love,
you who save by your right hand
those who take refuge in you from their foes.
Keep me as the apple of your eye;
hide me in the shadow of your wings
from the wicked who assail me,
from my mortal enemies who surround me.

Psalm 17:1-9

I urge, then, first of all, that requests, prayers, intercession and thanksgiving be made for everyone—for kings and all those in authority, that we may live peaceful and quiet lives in all godliness and holiness. This is good, and pleases God our Saviour, who wants all men to be saved and to come to a knowledge of the truth. For there is one God and one mediator between God and men, the man Christ Jesus, who gave himself as a ransom for all men—the testimony given in its proper time. And for this purpose I was appointed a herald and an apostle—I am telling the truth, I am not lying—and a teacher of the true faith to the Gentiles.

I want men everywhere to lift up holy hands in prayer, without anger or disputing.

1 Timothy 2:1-8

Confession

Blessed is he
whose transgressions are forgiven,
whose sins are covered.
Blessed is the man
whose sin the LORD does not count against him
and in whose spirit is no deceit.
When I kept silent,
my bones wasted away
through my groaning all day long.
For day and night
your hand was heavy upon me;
my strength was sapped
as in the heat of summer. Selah
Then I acknowledged my sin to you
and did not cover up my iniquity.
I said, "I will confess
my transgressions to the LORD"–
and you forgave
the guilt of my sin. Selah

Psalm 32:1-5

That which was from the beginning, which we have heard, which we have seen with our eyes, which we have looked at and our hands have touched—this we proclaim concerning the Word of life. The life appeared; we have seen it and testify to it, and we proclaim to you the eternal life, which was with the Father and has appeared to us. We proclaim to you what we have seen and heard, so that you also may have fellowship with us. And our fellowship is with the Father and with his Son, Jesus Christ. We write this to make our joy complete.

This is the message we have heard from him and declare to you: God is light; in him there is no darkness at all. If we claim to have fellowship with him yet walk in the darkness, we lie and do not live by the truth. But if we walk in the light, as he is in the light, we have fellowship with one another, and the blood of Jesus, his Son, purifies us from all sin.

If we claim to be without sin, we deceive ourselves and the truth is not in us. If we confess our sins, he is faithful and just and will forgive us our sins and purify us from all unrighteousness. If we claim we have not sinned, we make him out to be a liar and his word has no place in our lives.

1 John 1:1-10

Preservation

My dear brothers, take note of this: Everyone should be quick to listen, slow to speak and slow to become angry, for man's anger does not bring about the righteous life that God desires. Therefore, get rid of all moral filth and the evil that is so prevalent, and humbly accept the word planted in you, which can save you.

Do not merely listen to the word, and so deceive yourselves. Do what it says. Anyone who listens to the word but does not do what it says is like a man who looks at his face in a mirror and, after looking at himself, goes away and immediately forgets what he looks like. But the man who looks intently into the perfect law that gives freedom, and continues to do this, not forgetting what he has heard, but doing it - he will be blessed in what he does.

If anyone considers himself religious and yet does not keep a tight rein on his tongue, he deceives himself and his religion is worthless. Religion that God our Father accepts as pure and faultless is this: to look after orphans and widows in their distress and to keep oneself from being polluted by the world.

James 1:19-27

Madeleine Lemaire, "Roses"

Renewal

The ark of the LORD remained in the house of Obed-Edom the Gittite for three months, and the LORD blessed him and his entire household. Now King David was told, "The LORD has blessed the household of Obed-Edom and everything he has, because of the ark of God." So David went down and brought up the ark of God from the house of Obed-Edom to the City of David with rejoicing. When those who were carrying the ark of the LORD had taken six steps, he sacrificed a bull and a fattened calf. David, wearing a linen ephod, danced before the LORD with all his might, while he and the entire house of Israel brought up the ark of the LORD with shouts and the sound of trumpets.

As the ark of the LORD was entering the City of David, Michal daughter of Saul watched from a window. And when she saw King David leaping and dancing before the LORD, she despised him in her heart.

2 Samuel 6:11-16

Sing to the LORD a new song,
his praise from the ends of the earth,
you who go down to the sea, and all that is in it,
you islands, and all who live in them.
Let the desert and its towns raise their voices;
let the settlements where Kedar lives rejoice.
Let the people of Sela sing for joy;
let them shout from the mountaintops.
Let them give glory to the LORD
and proclaim his praise in the islands.
The LORD will march out like a mighty man,
like a warrior he will stir up his zeal;
with a shout he will raise the battle cry
and will triumph over his enemies.
For a long time I have kept silent,
I have been quiet and held myself back.
But now, like a woman in childbirth,
I cry out, I gasp and pant.
I will lay waste the mountains and hills
and dry up all their vegetation;
I will turn rivers into islands
and dry up the pools.
I will lead the blind by ways they have not known,
along unfamiliar paths I will guide them.

Isaiah 42:10-16

Faithfulness

Give thanks to the LORD, for he is good.
His love endures for ever.
Give thanks to the God of gods.
His love endures for ever.
Give thanks to the Lord of lords: His love endures for ever.
to him who alone does great wonders,
His love endures for ever.
who by his understanding made the heavens,
His love endures for ever.
who spread out the earth upon the waters,
His love endures for ever.
who made the great lights—
His love endures for ever.
the sun to govern the day,
His love endures for ever.
the moon and stars to govern the night;
His love endures for ever.

Psalm 136:1-9

Because of the LORD's great love we are not consumed,
for his compassions never fail.
They are new every morning;
great is your faithfulness.
I say to myself, "The LORD is my portion;
therefore I will wait for him."
The LORD is good to those whose hope is in him,
to the one who seeks him;
it is good to wait quietly
for the salvation of the LORD.
It is good for a man to bear the yoke
while he is young.
Let him sit alone in silence,
for the LORD has laid it on him.
Let him bury his face in the dust—
there may yet be hope.
Let him offer his cheek to one who would strike him,
and let him be filled with disgrace.
For men are not cast off
by the Lord for ever.
Though he brings grief, he will show compassion,
so great is his unfailing love.
For he does not willingly bring affliction
or grief to the children of men.

Lamentations 3:22-33

The Struggles of Praise

Trials

Rejection

Depression

Suffering

Grief and Mourning

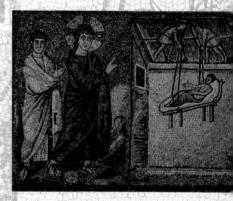

"The Paralytic left down through the Roof"

Trials

As the deer pants for streams of water,
so my soul pants for you, O God.
My soul thirsts for God, for the living God.
When can I go and meet with God?
My tears have been my food
day and night,
while men say to me all day long,
"Where is your God?"
These things I remember
as I pour out my soul:
how I used to go with the multitude,
leading the procession to the house of God,
with shouts of joy and thanksgiving
among the festive throng.
Why are you downcast, O my soul?
Why so disturbed within me?
Put your hope in God,
for I will yet praise him,
my Saviour and my God.
My soul is downcast within me;
therefore I will remember you
from the land of the Jordan,
the heights of Hermon—from Mount Mizar.

Psalm 42:1-6

By the rivers of Babylon we sat and wept
when we remembered Zion.
There on the poplars
we hung our harps,
for there our captors asked us for songs,
our tormentors demanded songs of joy;
they said, "Sing us one of the songs of Zion!"
How can we sing the songs of the LORD
while in a foreign land?
If I forget you, O Jerusalem,
may my right hand forget its skill.
May my tongue cling to the roof of my mouth
if I do not remember you,
if I do not consider Jerusalem
my highest joy.
Remember, O LORD, what the Edomites did
on the day Jerusalem fell.
"Tear it down," they cried,
"tear it down to its foundations!"
O Daughter of Babylon, doomed to destruction,
happy is he who repays you
for what you have done to us—
he who seizes your infants
and dashes them against the rocks.

Psalm 137:1-9

James Abbott McNeill Whistler, "Nocturne, Blue and Silver: Battersea Reach"

Rejection

My God, my God, why have you forsaken me?
Why are you so far from saving me,
so far from the words of my groaning?
O my God, I cry out by day, but you do not answer,
by night, and am not silent.
Yet you are enthroned as the Holy One;
you are the praise of Israel.
In you our fathers put their trust;
they trusted and you delivered them.
They cried to you and were saved;
in you they trusted and were not disappointed.
But I am a worm and not a man,
scorned by men and despised by the people.
All who see me mock me;
they hurl insults, shaking their heads:
"He trusts in the LORD;
let the LORD rescue him.
Let him deliver him,
since he delights in him."
Yet you brought me out of the womb;
you made me trust in you
even at my mother's breast.
From birth I was cast upon you;
from my mother's womb you have been my God.

Psalm 22:1-11

47

From the sixth hour until the ninth hour darkness came over all the land. About the ninth hour Jesus cried out in a loud voice, "Eloi, Eloi, lama sabachthani?"–which means, "My God, my God, why have you forsaken me?"

When some of those standing there heard this, they said, "He's calling Elijah."

Immediately one of them ran and got a sponge. He filled it with wine vinegar, put it on a stick, and offered it to Jesus to drink. The rest said, "Now leave him alone. Let's see if Elijah comes to save him."

And when Jesus had cried out again in a loud voice, he gave up his spirit.

At that moment the curtain of the temple was torn in two from top to bottom. The earth shook and the rocks split. The tombs broke open and the bodies of many holy people who had died were raised to life. They came out of the tombs, and after Jesus' resurrection they went into the holy city and appeared to many people.

When the centurion and those with him who were guarding Jesus saw the earthquake and all that had happened, they were terrified, and exclaimed, "Surely he was the Son of God!"

Many women were there, watching from a distance. They had followed Jesus from Galilee to care for his needs. Among them were Mary Magdalene, Mary the mother of James and Joses, and the mother of Zebedee's sons.

Matthew 27:45-56

Depression

I am the man who has seen affliction
by the rod of his wrath.
He has driven me away and made me walk
in darkness rather than light;
indeed, he has turned his hand against me
again and again, all day long.
He has made my skin and my flesh grow old
and has broken my bones.
He has besieged me and surrounded me
with bitterness and hardship.
He has made me dwell in darkness
like those long dead.
He has walled me in so that I cannot escape;
he has weighed me down with chains.
Even when I call out or cry for help,
he shuts out my prayer.
He has barred my way with blocks of stone;
he has made my paths crooked.
Like a bear lying in wait,
like a lion in hiding,
he dragged me from the path and mangled me
and left me without help.
He drew his bow
and made me the target for his arrows.

Lamentations 3:1-12

The enemy pursues me,
he crushes me to the ground;
he makes me dwell in darkness
like those long dead.
So my spirit grows faint within me;
my heart within me is dismayed.
I remember the days of long ago;
I meditate on all your works
and consider what your hands have done.
I spread out my hands to you;
my soul thirsts for you like a parched land. Selah
Answer me quickly, O LORD;
my spirit fails.
Do not hide your face from me
or I will be like those who go down to the pit.
Let the morning bring me word of your unfailing love,
for I have put my trust in you.
Show me the way I should go,
for to you I lift up my soul.
Rescue me from my enemies, O LORD,
for I hide myself in you.
Teach me to do your will,
for you are my God;
may your good Spirit lead me on level ground.

Psalm 143:3-10

Suffering

If only my anguish could be weighed
and all my misery be placed on the scales!
It would surely outweigh the sand of the seas—
no wonder my words have been impetuous.
The arrows of the Almighty are in me,
my spirit drinks in their poison;
God's terrors are marshalled against me.
Does a wild donkey bray when it has grass,
or an ox bellow when it has fodder?
Is tasteless food eaten without salt,
or is there flavour in the white of an egg?
I refuse to touch it; such food makes me ill.
Oh, that I might have my request,
that God would grant what I hope for,
that God would be willing to crush me,
to let loose his hand and cut me off!
Then I would still have this consolation—
my joy in unrelenting pain—
that I had not denied the words of the Holy One.
What strength do I have, that I should still hope?
What prospects, that I should be patient?
Do I have the strength of stone? Is my flesh bronze?
Do I have any power to help myself,
now that success has been driven from me?

Job 6:2-13

Princes have been hung up by their hands;
elders are shown no respect.
Young men toil at the millstones;
boys stagger under loads of wood.
The elders are gone from the city gate;
the young men have stopped their music.
Joy is gone from our hearts;
our dancing has turned to mourning.
The crown has fallen from our head.
Woe to us, for we have sinned!
Because of this our hearts are faint;
because of these things our eyes grow dim
for Mount Zion, which lies desolate,
with jackals prowling over it.
You, O LORD, reign for ever;
your throne endures from generation to generation.
Why do you always forget us?
Why do you forsake us so long?
Restore us to yourself, O LORD, that we may return;
renew our days as of old
unless you have utterly rejected us
and are angry with us beyond measure.

Lamentations 5:12-22

Grief and Mourning

O mountains of Gilboa,
may you have neither dew nor rain,
nor fields that yield offerings of grain.
For there the shield of the mighty was defiled,
the shield of Saul—no longer rubbed with oil.
From the blood of the slain, from the flesh of the mighty,
the bow of Jonathan did not turn back,
the sword of Saul did not return unsatisfied.
Saul and Jonathan—
in life they were loved and gracious,
and in death they were not parted.
They were swifter than eagles,
they were stronger than lions.
O daughters of Israel, weep for Saul,
who clothed you in scarlet and finery,
who adorned your garments with ornaments of gold.
How the mighty have fallen in battle!
Jonathan lies slain on your heights.
I grieve for you, Jonathan my brother;
you were very dear to me.
Your love for me was wonderful,
more wonderful than that of women.
How the mighty have fallen!
The weapons of war have perished!

2 Samuel 1:21-27

The Liberation of Praise

Reconciliation

Peace

Joy

Hope

Freedom

"The Healing of the Madman"

Reconciliation

Yet if there is an angel on his side
as a mediator, one out of a thousand,
to tell a man what is right for him,
to be gracious to him and say,
'Spare him from going down to the pit;
I have found a ransom for him'–
then his flesh is renewed like a child's;
it is restored as in the days of his youth.
He prays to God and finds favour with him,
he sees God's face and shouts for joy;
he is restored by God to his righteous state.
Then he comes to men and says,
'I have sinned, and perverted what was right,
but I did not get what I deserved.
He redeemed my soul from going down to the pit,
and I shall live to enjoy the light.'
God does all these things to a man–
twice, even three times–
to turn back his soul from the pit,
that the light of life may shine on him.

Job 33:23-30

Since, then, we know what it is to fear the Lord, we try to persuade men. What we are is plain to God, and I hope it is also plain to your conscience. We are not trying to commend ourselves to you again, but are giving you an opportunity to take pride in us, so that you can answer those who take pride in what is seen rather than in what is in the heart. If we are out of our mind, it is for the sake of God; if we are in our right mind, it is for you. For Christ's love compels us, because we are convinced that one died for all, and therefore all died. And he died for all, that those who live should no longer live for themselves but for him who died for them and was raised again.

So from now on we regard no-one from a worldly point of view. Though we once regarded Christ in this way, we do so no longer. Therefore, if anyone is in Christ, he is a new creation; the old has gone, the new has come! All this is from God, who reconciled us to himself through Christ and gave us the ministry of reconciliation: that God was reconciling the world to himself in Christ, not counting men's sins against them. And he has committed to us the message of reconciliation. We are therefore Christ's ambassadors, as though God were making his appeal through us. We implore you on Christ's behalf: Be reconciled to God. God made him who had no sin to be sin for us, so that in him we might become the righteousness of God.

2 Corinthians 5:11-21

Peace

Now the Spirit of the LORD had departed from Saul, and an evil spirit from the LORD tormented him.

Saul's attendants said to him, "See, an evil spirit from God is tormenting you. Let our lord command his servants here to search for someone who can play the harp. He will play when the evil spirit from God comes upon you, and you will feel better."

So Saul said to his attendants, "Find someone who plays well and bring him to me."

One of the servants answered, "I have seen a son of Jesse of Bethlehem who knows how to play the harp. He is a brave man and a warrior. He speaks well and is a fine-looking man. And the LORD is with him."

Then Saul sent messengers to Jesse and said, "Send me your son David, who is with the sheep." So Jesse took a donkey loaded with bread, a skin of wine and a young goat and sent them with his son David to Saul.

David came to Saul and entered his service. Saul liked him very much, and David became one of his armour-bearers. Then Saul sent word to Jesse, saying, "Allow David to remain in my service, for I am pleased with him."

Whenever the spirit from God came upon Saul, David would take his harp and play. Then relief would come to Saul; he would feel better, and the evil spirit would leave him.

1 Samuel 16:14-23

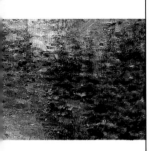

"Build up, build up, prepare the road!
Remove the obstacles out of the way of my people."
For this is what the high and lofty One says—
he who lives for ever, whose name is holy:
"I live in a high and holy place,
but also with him who is contrite and lowly in spirit,
to revive the spirit of the lowly
and to revive the heart of the contrite.
I will not accuse for ever,
nor will I always be angry,
for then the spirit of man would grow faint before me—
the breath of man that I have created.
I was enraged by his sinful greed;
I punished him, and hid my face in anger,
yet he kept on in his wilful ways.
I have seen his ways, but I will heal him;
I will guide him and restore comfort to him,
creating praise on the lips of the mourners in Israel.
Peace, peace, to those far and near,"
says the LORD. "And I will heal them."
But the wicked are like the tossing sea,
which cannot rest,
whose waves cast up mire and mud.
"There is no peace," says my God, "for the wicked."

Isaiah 57:14-21

Joy

Sing joyfully to the LORD, you righteous;
it is fitting for the upright to praise him.
Praise the LORD with the harp;
make music to him on the ten-stringed lyre.
Sing to him a new song;
play skilfully, and shout for joy.
For the word of the LORD is right and true;
he is faithful in all he does.
The LORD loves righteousness and justice;
the earth is full of his unfailing love.
By the word of the LORD were the heavens made,
their starry host by the breath of his mouth.
He gathers the waters of the sea into jars;
he puts the deep into storehouses.
Let all the earth fear the LORD;
let all the people of the world revere him.
For he spoke, and it came to be;
he commanded, and it stood firm.
The LORD foils the plans of the nations;
he thwarts the purposes of the peoples.
But the plans of the LORD stand firm for ever,
the purposes of his heart through all generations.
Blessed is the nation whose God is the LORD,
the people he chose for his inheritance.

Psalm 33:1-12

Claude Monet, "Poplars on the Epte"

Sing, O Daughter of Zion;
shout aloud, O Israel!
Be glad and rejoice with all your heart,
O Daughter of Jerusalem!
The LORD has taken away your punishment,
he has turned back your enemy.
The LORD, the King of Israel, is with you;
never again will you fear any harm.
On that day they will say to Jerusalem,
"Do not fear, O Zion;
do not let your hands hang limp.
The LORD your God is with you,
he is mighty to save.
He will take great delight in you,
he will quiet you with his love,
he will rejoice over you with singing."

Zephaniah 3:14-17

Hope

Praise be to the God and Father of our Lord Jesus Christ! In his great mercy he has given us new birth into a living hope through the resurrection of Jesus Christ from the dead, and into an inheritance that can never perish, spoil or fade—kept in heaven for you, who through faith are shielded by God's power until the coming of the salvation that is ready to be revealed in the last time. In this you greatly rejoice, though now for a little while you may have had to suffer grief in all kinds of trials. These have come so that your faith—of greater worth than gold, which perishes even though refined by fire—may be proved genuine and may result in praise, glory and honour when Jesus Christ is revealed. Though you have not seen him, you love him; and even though you do not see him now, you believe in him and are filled with an inexpressible and glorious joy, for you are receiving the goal of your faith, the salvation of your souls.

1 Peter 1:3-9

Freedom

Joshua got up early the next morning and the priests took up the ark of the LORD. The seven priests carrying the seven trumpets went forward, marching before the ark of the LORD and blowing the trumpets. The armed men went ahead of them and the rear guard followed the ark of the LORD, while the trumpets kept sounding. So on the second day they marched around the city once and returned to the camp. They did this for six days.

On the seventh day, they got up at daybreak and marched around the city seven times in the same manner, except that on that day they circled the city seven times. The seventh time around, when the priests sounded the trumpet blast, Joshua commanded the people, "Shout! For the LORD has given you the city! The city and all that is in it are to be devoted to the LORD. Only Rahab the prostitute and all who are with her in her house shall be spared, because she hid the spies we sent. But keep away from the devoted things, so that you will not bring about your own destruction by taking any of them. Otherwise you will make the camp of Israel liable to destruction and bring trouble on it. All the silver and gold and the articles of bronze and iron are sacred to the LORD and must go into his treasury."

When the trumpets sounded, the people shouted, and at the sound of the trumpet, when the people gave a loud shout, the wall collapsed; so every man charged straight in, and they took the city.

Joshua 6:12-20

About midnight Paul and Silas were praying and singing hymns to God, and the other prisoners were listening to them. Suddenly there was such a violent earthquake that the foundations of the prison were shaken. At once all the prison doors flew open, and everybody's chains came loose. The jailer woke up, and when he saw the prison doors open, he drew his sword and was about to kill himself because he thought the prisoners had escaped. But Paul shouted, "Don't harm yourself! We are all here!"

The jailer called for lights, rushed in and fell trembling before Paul and Silas. He then brought them out and asked, "Sirs, what must I do to be saved?"

They replied, "Believe in the Lord Jesus, and you will be saved—you and your household." Then they spoke the word of the Lord to him and to all the others in his house. At that hour of the night the jailer took them and washed their wounds; then immediately he and all his family were baptised. The jailer brought them into his house and set a meal before them; he was filled with joy because he had come to believe in God - he and his whole family.

Acts 16:25-34

The Spirit of Praise

Powerlessness

Submission

Refuge

Truth

Faith

"The Samaritan Woman at the Well"

Powerlessness

Hasten, O God, to save me;
O LORD, come quickly to help me.
May those who seek my life
be put to shame and confusion;
may all who desire my ruin
be turned back in disgrace.
May those who say to me, "Aha! Aha!"
turn back because of their shame.
But may all who seek you
rejoice and be glad in you;
may those who love your salvation always say,
"Let God be exalted!"
Yet I am poor and needy;
come quickly to me, O God.
You are my help and my deliverer;
O LORD, do not delay.

Psalm 70:1-5

"O afflicted city, lashed by storms and not comforted,
I will build you with stones of turquoise,
your foundations with sapphires.
I will make your battlements of rubies,
your gates of sparkling jewels,
and all your walls of precious stones.
All your sons will be taught by the LORD,
and great will be your children's peace.
In righteousness you will be established:
Tyranny will be far from you;
you will have nothing to fear.
Terror will be far removed;
it will not come near you.
If anyone does attack you, it will not be my doing;
whoever attacks you will surrender to you.
"See, it is I who created the blacksmith
who fans the coals into flame
and forges a weapon fit for its work.
And it is I who have created the destroyer to work havoc;
no weapon forged against you will prevail,
and you will refute every tongue that accuses you.
This is the heritage of the servants of the LORD,
and this is their vindication from me,"
declares the LORD.

Isaiah 54:11-17

Adelsteen Normann, "A Fjord Steamer"

Submission

Come, let us sing for
joy to the LORD;
let us shout aloud to the Rock of our salvation.
Let us come before him with thanksgiving
and extol him with music and song.
For the LORD is the great God,
the great King above all gods.
In his hand are the depths of the earth,
and the mountain peaks belong to him.
The sea is his, for he made it,
and his hands formed the dry land.
Come, let us bow down in worship,
let us kneel before the LORD our Maker;
for he is our God and we are the people of his pasture,
the flock under his care.
Today, if you hear his voice,
do not harden your hearts as you did at Meribah,
as you did that day at Massah in the desert,
where your fathers tested and tried me,
though they had seen what I did.
For forty years I was angry with that generation;
I said, "They are a people whose hearts go astray,
and they have not known my ways."
So I declared on oath in my anger,
"They shall never enter my rest."

Psalm 95:1-11

Ascribe to the LORD, 0 families of nations,
ascribe to the LORD glory and strength,
ascribe to the LORD the glory due to his name.
Bring an offering and come before him;
worship the LORD in the splendour of his holiness.
Tremble before him, all the earth!
The world is firmly established; it cannot be moved.
Let the heavens rejoice, let the earth be glad;
let them say among the nations, "The LORD reigns!"
Let the sea resound, and all that is in it;
let the fields be jubilant, and everything in them!
Then the trees of the forest will sing,
they will sing for joy before the LORD,
for he comes to judge the earth.
Give thanks to the LORD, for he is good;
his love endures for ever.
Cry out, "Save us, 0 God our Saviour;
gather us and deliver us from the nations,
that we may give thanks to your holy name,
that we may glory in your praise."
Praise be to the LORD, the God of Israel,
from everlasting to everlasting.
Then all the people said "Amen" and "Praise the LORD."

1 Chronicles 16:28-36

Refuge

In you, O LORD, I have taken refuge;
let me never be put to shame.
Rescue me and deliver me in your righteousness;
turn your ear to me and save me.
Be my rock of refuge,
to which I can always go;
give the command to save me,
for you are my rock and my fortress.
Deliver me, O my God, from the hand of the wicked,
from the grasp of evil and cruel men.
For you have been my hope, O Sovereign LORD,
my confidence since my youth.
From my birth I have relied on you;
you brought me forth from my mother's womb.
I will ever praise you.
I have become like a portent to many,
but you are my strong refuge.
My mouth is filled with your praise,
declaring your splendour all day long.

Psalm 71:1-8

Have mercy on me, O God, have mercy on me,
for in you my soul takes refuge.
I will take refuge in the shadow of your wings
until the disaster has passed.
I cry out to God Most High,
to God, who fulfils his purpose for me.
He sends from heaven and saves me,
rebuking those who hotly pursue me; Selah
God sends his love and his faithfulness.
I am in the midst of lions;
I lie among ravenous beasts—
men whose teeth are spears and arrows,
whose tongues are sharp swords.
Be exalted, O God, above the heavens;
let your glory be over all the earth.
They spread a net for my feet—
I was bowed down in distress.
They dug a pit in my path—
but they have fallen into it themselves. Selah
My heart is steadfast, O God,
my heart is steadfast;
I will sing and make music.
Awake, my soul! Awake, harp and lyre!
I will awaken the dawn.

Psalm 57:1-8

Truth

My son, do not forget my teaching,
but keep my commands in your heart,
for they will prolong your life many years
and bring you prosperity.
Let love and faithfulness never leave you;
bind them around your neck,
write them on the tablet of your heart.
Then you will win favour and a good name
in the sight of God and man.
Trust in the LORD with all your heart
and lean not on your own understanding;
in all your ways acknowledge him,
and he will make your paths straight.
Do not be wise in your own eyes;
fear the LORD and shun evil.
This will bring health to your body
and nourishment to your bones.
Honour the LORD with your wealth,
with the firstfruits of all your crops;
then your barns will be filled to overflowing,
and your vats will brim over with new wine.

Proverbs 3:1-10

He told her, "Go, call your husband and come back."

"I have no husband," she replied.

Jesus said to her, "You are right when you say you have no husband. The fact is, you have had five husbands, and the man you now have is not your husband. What you have just said is quite true.

"Sir," the woman said, "I can see that you are a prophet. Our fathers worshipped on this mountain, but you Jews claim that the place where we must worship is in Jerusalem."

Jesus declared, "Believe me, woman, a time is coming when you will worship the Father neither on this mountain nor in Jerusalem. You Samaritans worship what you do not know; we worship what we do know, for salvation is from the Jews. Yet a time is coming and has now come when the true worshippers will worship the Father in spirit and truth, for they are the kind of worshippers the Father seeks. God is spirit, and his worshippers must worship in spirit and in truth."

The woman said, "I know that Messiah" (called Christ) "is coming. When he comes, he will explain everything to us."

Then Jesus declared, "I who speak to you am he."

John 4:16-26

Faith

The Amalekites came and attacked the Israelites at Rephidim. Moses said to Joshua, "Choose some of our men and go out to fight the Amalekites. Tomorrow I will stand on top of the hill with the staff of God in my hands."

So Joshua fought the Amalekites as Moses had ordered, and Moses, Aaron and Hur went to the top of the hill. As long as Moses held up his hands, the Israelites were winning, but whenever he lowered his hands, the Amalekites were winning. When Moses' hands grew tired, they took a stone and put it under him and he sat on it. Aaron and Hur held his hands up—one on one side, one on the other—so that his hands remained steady till sunset. So Joshua overcame the Amalekite army with the sword.

Then the LORD said to Moses, "Write this on a scroll as something to be remembered and make sure that Joshua hears it, because I will completely blot out the memory of Amalek from under heaven."

Moses built an altar and called it The LORD is my Banner. He said, "For hands were lifted up to the throne of the LORD. The LORD will be at war against the Amalekites from generation to generation."

Exodus 17:8-16

The Mystery of Praise

Purification

Revelation

The Son of God –
Jesus Christ

The Holy Spirit

Anoiting

"Noah releasing the white Dove"

Purification

You have wearied the LORD with your words.

"How have we wearied him?" you ask.

By saying, "All who do evil are good in the eyes of the LORD, and he is pleased with them" or "Where is the God of justice?"

"See, I will send my messenger, who will prepare the way before me. Then suddenly the Lord you are seeking will come to his temple; the messenger of the covenant, whom you desire, will come," says the LORD Almighty.

But who can endure the day of his coming? Who can stand when he appears? For he will be like a refiner's fire or a launderer's soap. He will sit as a refiner and purifier of silver; he will purify the Levites and refine them like gold and silver. Then the LORD will have men who will bring offerings in righteousness, and the offerings of Judah and Jerusalem will be acceptable to the LORD, as in days gone by, as in former years.

Malachi 2:17-3:4

It was just before the Passover Feast. Jesus knew that the time had come for him to leave this world and go to the Father. Having loved his own who were in the world, he now showed them the full extent of his love.

The evening meal was being served, and the devil had already prompted Judas Iscariot, son of Simon, to betray Jesus. Jesus knew that the Father had put all things under his power, and that he had come from God and was returning to God; so he got up from the meal, took off his outer clothing, and wrapped a towel round his waist. After that, he poured water into a basin and began to wash his disciples' feet, drying them with the towel that was wrapped round him.

He came to Simon Peter, who said to him, "Lord, are you going to wash my feet?"

Jesus replied, "You do not realise now what I am doing, but later you will understand." "No," said Peter, "you shall never wash my feet."

Jesus answered, "Unless I wash you, you have no part with me."

"Then, Lord," Simon Peter replied, "not just my feet but my hands and my head as well!"

Jesus answered, "A person who has had a bath needs only to wash his feet; his whole body is clean. And you are clean, though not every one of you." For he knew who was going to betray him, and that was why he said not every one was clean.

John 13:1-11

Revelation

In the centre, around the throne, were four living creatures, and they were covered with eyes, in front and behind. The first living creature was like a lion, the second was like an ox, the third had a face like a man, the fourth was like a flying eagle. Each of the four living creatures had six wings and was covered with eyes all around, even under his wings. Day and night they never stop saying:

"Holy, holy, holy
is the Lord God Almighty,
who was, and is, and is to come."

Whenever the living creatures give glory, honour and thanks to him who sits on the throne and who lives for ever and ever, the twenty-four elders fall down before him who sits on the throne, and worship him who lives for ever and ever. They lay their crowns before the throne and say:

"You are worthy, our Lord and God,
to receive glory and honour and power,
for you created all things,
and by your will they were created
and have their being."

Revelation 4:6-11

The Son of God, Jesus Christ

When Jesus came to the region of Caesarea Philippi, he asked his disciples, "Who do people say the Son of Man is?"

They replied, "Some say John the Baptist; others say Elijah; and still others, Jeremiah or one of the prophets."

"But what about you?" he asked. "Who do you say I am?"

Simon Peter answered, "You are the Christ, the Son of the living God."

Jesus replied, "Blessed are you, Simon son of Jonah, for this was not revealed to you by man, but by my Father in heaven. And I tell you that you are Peter, and on this rock I will build my church, and the gates of Hades will not overcome it. I will give you the keys of the kingdom of heaven; whatever you bind on earth will be bound in heaven, and whatever you loose on earth will be loosed in heaven." Then he warned his disciples not to tell anyone that he was the Christ.

Matthew 16:13-20

Everyone who believes that Jesus is the Christ is born of God, and everyone who loves the father loves his child as well. This is how we know that we love the children of God: by loving God and carrying out his commands. This is love for God: to obey his commands. And his commands are not burdensome, for everyone born of God overcomes the world. This is the victory that has overcome the world, even our faith. Who is it that overcomes the world? Only he who believes that Jesus is the Son of God. This is the one who came by water and blood–Jesus Christ. He did not come by water only, but by water and blood. And it is the Spirit who testifies, because the Spirit is the truth. For there are three that testify: the Spirit, the water and the blood; and the three are in agreement. We accept man's testimony, but God's testimony is greater because it is the testimony of God, which he has given about his Son. Anyone who believes in the Son of God has this testimony in his heart. Anyone who does not believe God has made him out to be a liar, because he has not believed the testimony God has given about his Son. And this is the testimony: God has given us eternal life, and this life is in his Son. He who has the Son has life; he who does not have the Son of God does not have life.

1 John 5:1-12

The Holy Spirit

You, however, are controlled not by the sinful nature but by the Spirit, if the Spirit of God lives in you. And if anyone does not have the Spirit of Christ, he does not belong to Christ. But if Christ is in you, your body is dead because of sin, yet your spirit is alive because of righteousness. And if the Spirit of him who raised Jesus from the dead is living in you, he who raised Christ from the dead will also give life to your mortal bodies through his Spirit, who lives in you.

Therefore, brothers, we have an obligation—but it is not to the sinful nature, to live according to it. For if you live according to the sinful nature, you will die; but if by the Spirit you put to death the misdeeds of the body, you will live, because those who are led by the Spirit of God are sons of God. For you did not receive a spirit that makes you a slave again to fear, but you received the Spirit of sonship. And by him we cry, "Abba, Father." The Spirit himself testifies with our spirit that we are God's children. Now if we are children, then we are heirs—heirs of God and co-heirs with Christ, if indeed we share in his sufferings in order that we may also share in his glory.

Romans 8:9-17

Vilhelm Hammershøi, "Dust Motes dancing in Sunlight"

Follow the way of love and eagerly desire spiritual gifts, especially the gift of prophecy. For anyone who speaks in a tongue does not speak to men but to God. Indeed, no-one understands him; he utters mysteries with his spirit. But everyone who prophesies speaks to men for their strengthening, encouragement and comfort. He who speaks in a tongue edifies himself, but he who prophesies edifies the church. I would like every one of you to speak in tongues, but I would rather have you prophesy. He who prophesies is greater than one who speaks in tongues, unless he interprets, so that the church may be edified.

Now, brothers, if I come to you and speak in tongues, what good will I be to you, unless I bring you some revelation or knowledge or prophecy or word of instruction? Even in the case of lifeless things that make sounds, such as the flute or harp, how will anyone know what tune is being played unless there is a distinction in the notes? Again, if the trumpet does not sound a clear call, who will get ready for battle? So it is with you. Unless you speak intelligible words with your tongue, how will anyone know what you are saying? You will just be speaking into the air. Undoubtedly there are all sorts of languages in the world, yet none of them is without meaning. If then I do not grasp the meaning of what someone is saying, I am a foreigner to the speaker, and he is a foreigner to me. So it is with you. Since you are eager to have spiritual gifts, try to excel in gifts that build up the church.

1 Corinthians 14:1-12

Anointing

For to us a child is born,
to us a son is given,
and the government will be on his shoulders.
And he will be called
Wonderful Counsellor, Mighty God,
Everlasting Father, Prince of Peace.
Of the increase of his government and peace
there will be no end.
He will reign on David's throne
and over his kingdom,
establishing and upholding it
with justice and righteousness
from that time on and for ever.
The zeal of the LORD Almighty
will accomplish this.

Isaiah 9:6-7

Then Samuel took a flask of oil and poured it on Saul's head and kissed him, saying, "Has not the LORD anointed you leader over his inheritance? When you leave me today, you will meet two men near Rachel's tomb, at Zelzah on the border of Benjamin. They will say to you, 'The donkeys you set out to look for have been found. And now your father has stopped thinking about them and is worried about you. He is asking, "What shall I do about my son?" '

"Then you will go on from there until you reach the great tree of Tabor. Three men going up to God at Bethel will meet you there. One will be carrying three young goats, another three loaves of bread, and another a skin of wine. They will greet you and offer you two loaves of bread, which you will accept from them.

"After that you will go to Gibeah of God, where there is a Philistine outpost. As you approach the town, you will meet a procession of prophets coming down from the high place with lyres, tambourines, flutes and harps being played before them, and they will be prophesying. The Spirit of the LORD will come upon you in power, and you will prophesy with them; and you will be changed into a different person. Once these signs are fulfilled, do whatever your hand finds to do, for God is with you.

"Go down ahead of me to Gilgal. I will surely come down to you to sacrifice burnt offerings and fellowship offerings, but you must wait seven days until I come to you and tell you what you are to do."

1 Samuel 10:1-8

The Fellowship of Praise

Unity

Redemption

Friendship

Family

Community

"The Last Supper"

Unity

Now the body is not made up of one part but of many. If the foot should say, "Because I am not a hand, I do not belong to the body," it would not for that reason cease to be part of the body. And if the ear should say, "Because I am not an eye, I do not belong to the body," it would not for that reason cease to be part of the body. If the whole body were an eye, where would the sense of hearing be? If the whole body were an ear, where would the sense of smell be? But in fact God has arranged the parts in the body, every one of them, just as he wanted them to be. If they were all one part, where would the body be? As it is, there are many parts, but one body.

The eye cannot say to the hand, "I don't need you!" And the head cannot say to the feet, "I don't need you!" On the contrary, those parts of the body that seem to be weaker are indispensable, and the parts that we think are less honourable we treat with special honour. And the parts that are unpresentable are treated with special modesty, while our presentable parts need no special treatment. But God has combined the members of the body and has given greater honour to the parts that lacked it, so that there should be no division in the body, but that its parts should have equal concern for each other. If one part suffers, every part suffers with it; if one part is honoured, every part rejoices with it.

1 Corinthians 12:14-26

Therefore, rid yourselves of all malice and all deceit, hypocrisy, envy, and slander of every kind. Like newborn babies, crave pure spiritual milk, so that by it you may grow up in your salvation, now that you have tasted that the Lord is good.

As you come to him, the living Stone–rejected by men but chosen by God and precious to him– you also, like living stones, are being built into a spiritual house to be a holy priesthood, offering spiritual sacrifices acceptable to God through Jesus Christ. For in Scripture it says:

"See, I lay a stone in Zion,

a chosen and precious cornerstone,

and the one who trusts in him

will never be put to shame." Now to you who believe, this stone is precious. But to those who do not believe,

"The stone the builders rejected

has become the capstone," and,

"A stone that causes men to stumble

and a rock that makes them fall."

They stumble because they disobey the message–which is also what they were destined for.

But you are a chosen people, a royal priesthood, a holy nation, a people belonging to God, that you may declare the praises of him who called you out of darkness into his wonderful light. Once you were not a people, but now you are the people of God; once you had not received mercy, but now you have received mercy.

1 Peter 2:1-10

Johannes Martin Grimelund, "Summer Morning at Molde"

Redemption

Who among the gods is like you, O LORD?
Who is like you -
majestic in holiness,
awesome in glory, working wonders?
You stretched out your right hand
and the earth swallowed them.
In your unfailing love you will lead
the people you have redeemed.
In your strength you will guide them
to your holy dwelling.
The nations will hear and tremble;
anguish will grip the people of Philistia.
The chiefs of Edom will be terrified,
the leaders of Moab will be seized with trembling,
the people of Canaan will melt away;
terror and dread will fall upon them.
By the power of your arm
they will be as still as a stone -
until your people pass by, O LORD,
until the people you bought pass by.
You will bring them in and plant them
on the mountain of your inheritance -
the place, O LORD, you made for your dwelling,
the sanctuary, O Lord, your hands established.

Exodus 15:11-17

In a desert land he found him,
in a barren and howling waste.
He shielded him and cared for him;
he guarded him as the apple of his eye,
like an eagle that stirs up its nest
and hovers over its young,
that spreads its wings to catch them
and carries them on its pinions.
The LORD alone led him;
no foreign god was with him.
He made him ride on the heights of the land
and fed him with the fruit of the fields.
He nourished him with honey from the rock,
and with oil from the flinty crag,
with curds and milk from herd and flock
and with fattened lambs and goats,
with choice rams of Bashan
and the finest grains of wheat.
You drank the foaming blood of the grape.

Deuteronomy 32:10-14

Friendship

Saul told his son Jonathan and all the attendants to kill David. But Jonathan was very fond of David and warned him, "My father Saul is looking for a chance to kill you. Be on your guard tomorrow morning; go into hiding and stay there. I will go out and stand with my father in the field where you are. I'll speak to him about you and will tell you what I find out."

Jonathan spoke well of David to Saul his father and said to him, "Let not the king do wrong to his servant David; he has not wronged you, and what he has done has benefited you greatly. He took his life in his hands when he killed the Philistine. The LORD won a great victory for all Israel, and you saw it and were glad. Why then would you do wrong to an innocent man like David by killing him for no reason?"

Saul listened to Jonathan and took this oath: "As surely as the LORD lives, David will not be put to death."

So Jonathan called David and told him the whole conversation. He brought him to Saul, and David was with Saul as before.

Once more war broke out, and David went out and fought the Philistines. He struck them with such force that they fled before him.

1 Samuel 19:1-8

Dear friends, let us love one another, for love comes from God. Everyone who loves has been born of God and knows God. Whoever does not love does not know God, because God is love. This is how God showed his love among us: He sent his one and only Son into the world that we might live through him. This is love: not that we loved God, but that he loved us and sent his Son as an atoning sacrifice for our sins. Dear friends, since God so loved us, we also ought to love one another. No-one has ever seen God; but if we love one another, God lives in us and his love is made complete in us.

We know that we live in him and he in us, because he has given us of his Spirit. And we have seen and testify that the Father has sent his Son to be the Saviour of the world. If anyone acknowledges that Jesus is the Son of God, God lives in him and he in God. And so we know and rely on the love God has for us.

1 John 4:7-16

Family

Hear, O Israel: The LORD our God, the LORD is one. Love the LORD your God with all your heart and with all your soul and with all your strength. These commandments that I give you today are to be upon your hearts. Impress them on your children. Talk about them when you sit at home and when you walk along the road, when you lie down and when you get up. Tie them as symbols on your hands and bind them on your foreheads. Write them on the door-frames of your houses and on your gates.

When the LORD your God brings you into the land he swore to your fathers, to Abraham, Isaac and Jacob, to give you - a land with large, flourishing cities you did not build, houses filled with all kinds of good things you did not provide, wells you did not dig, and vineyards and olive groves you did not plant - then when you eat and are satisfied, be careful that you do not forget the LORD, who brought you out of Egypt, out of the land of slavery.

Fear the LORD your God, serve him only and take your oaths in his name.

Deuteronomy 6:4-13

Community

As a prisoner for the Lord, then, I urge you to live a life worthy of the calling you have received. Be completely humble and gentle; be patient, bearing with one another in love. Make every effort to keep the unity of the Spirit through the bond of peace. There is one body and one Spirit - just as you were called to one hope when you were called - one Lord, one faith, one baptism; one God and Father of all, who is over all and through all and in all.

Ephesians 4:1-6

Therefore, as God's chosen people, holy and dearly loved, clothe yourselves with compassion, kindness, humility, gentleness and patience. Bear with each other and forgive whatever grievances you may have against one another. Forgive as the Lord forgave you. And over all these virtues put on love, which binds them all together in perfect unity.

Let the peace of Christ rule in your hearts, since as members of one body you were called to peace. And be thankful. Let the word of Christ dwell in you richly as you teach and admonish one another with all wisdom, and as you sing psalms, hymns and spiritual songs with gratitude in your hearts to God. And whatever you do, whether in word or deed, do it all in the name of the Lord Jesus, giving thanks to God the Father through him.

Colossians 3:12-17

This is the message you heard from the beginning: We should love one another. Do not be like Cain, who belonged to the evil one and murdered his brother. And why did he murder him? Because his own actions were evil and his brother's were righteous. Do not be surprised, my brothers, if the world hates you. We know that we have passed from death to life, because we love our brothers. Anyone who does not love remains in death. Anyone who hates his brother is a murderer, and you know that no murderer has eternal life in him.

This is how we know what love is: Jesus Christ laid down his life for us. And we ought to lay down our lives for our brothers. If anyone has material possessions and sees his brother in need but has no pity on him, how can the love of God be in him? Dear children, let us not love with words or tongue but with actions and in truth. This then is how we know that we belong to the truth, and how we set our hearts at rest in his presence whenever our hearts condemn us. For God is greater than our hearts, and he knows everything.

Dear friends, if our hearts do not condemn us, we have confidence before God and receive from him anything we ask, because we obey his commands and do what pleases him. And this is his command: to believe in the name of his Son, Jesus Christ, and to love one another as he commanded us. Those who obey his commands live in him, and he in them. And this is how we know that he lives in us: We know it by the Spirit he gave us.

1 John 3:11-24

"Detail of the Greek Fret"

Moses' Song

See now that I myself am He!
There is no god besides me.
I put to death and I bring to life,
I have wounded and I will heal,
and no-one can deliver out of my hand.
I lift my hand to heaven and declare:
As surely as I live for ever,
when I sharpen my flashing sword
and my hand grasps it in judgment,
I will take vengeance on my adversaries
and repay those who hate me.
I will make my arrows drunk with blood,
while my sword devours flesh:
the blood of the slain and the captives,
the heads of the enemy leaders."
Rejoice, O nations, with his people,
for he will avenge the blood of his servants;
he will take vengeance on his enemies
and make atonement for his land and people.

Deuteronomy 32:36-43

Deborah's Song

When the princes in Israel take the lead,
when the people willingly offer themselves -
praise the LORD!
Hear this, you kings! Listen, you rulers!
I will sing to the LORD, I will sing;
I will make music to the LORD, the God of Israel.
O LORD, when you went out from Seir,
when you marched from the land of Edom,
the earth shook, the heavens poured,
the clouds poured down water.
The mountains quaked before the LORD, the One of Sinai,
before the LORD, the God of Israel.
In the days of Shamgar son of Anath,
in the days of Jael, the roads were abandoned;
travellers took to winding paths.
Village life in Israel ceased,
ceased until I, Deborah, arose,
arose a mother in Israel.
When they chose new gods,
war came to the city gates,
and not a shield or spear was seen
among forty thousand in Israel.
My heart is with Israel's princes,
with the willing volunteers among the people.
Praise the LORD!

You who ride on white donkeys,
sitting on your saddle blankets,
and you who walk along the road,
consider the voice of the singers at the watering places.
They recite the righteous acts of the LORD,
the righteous acts of his warriors in Israel.
Then the people of the LORD
went down to the city gates.
'Wake up, wake up, Deborah!
Wake up, wake up, break out in song!
Arise, O Barak!
Take captive your captives, O son of Abinoam.'
Then the men who were left
came down to the nobles;
the people of the LORD
came to me with the mighty.
Some came from Ephraim, whose roots were in Amalek;
Benjamin was with the people who followed you.
From Makir captains came down,
from Zebulun those who bear a commander's staff.
The princes of Issachar were with Deborah;
yes, Issachar was with Barak,
rushing after him into the valley.

Judges 5:1-15

Hannah's Song

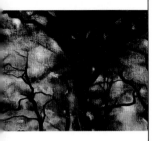

My heart rejoices in the LORD;
in the LORD my horn is lifted high.
My mouth boasts over my enemies,
for I delight in your deliverance.
There is no-one holy like the LORD;
there is no-one besides you;
there is no Rock like our God.
Do not keep talking so proudly
or let your mouth speak such arrogance,
for the LORD is a God who knows,
and by him deeds are weighed.
The bows of the warriors are broken,
but those who stumbled are armed with strength.
Those who were full hire themselves out for food,
but those who were hungry hunger no more.
She who was barren has borne seven children,
but she who has had many sons pines away.

The LORD brings death and makes alive;
he brings down to the grave and raises up.
The LORD sends poverty and wealth;
he humbles and he exalts.
He raises the poor from the dust
and lifts the needy from the ash heap;
he seats them with princes
and has them inherit a throne of honour.
For the foundations of the earth are the LORD's;
upon them he has set the world.
He will guard the feet of his saints,
but the wicked will be silenced in darkness.
It is not by strength that one prevails;
those who oppose the LORD will be shattered.
He will thunder against them from heaven;
the LORD will judge the ends of the earth.
He will give strength to his king
and exalt the horn of his anointed.

1 Samuel 2:1-10

David's Song

To the faithful you show yourself faithful,
to the blameless you show yourself blameless,
to the pure you show yourself pure,
but to the crooked you show yourself shrewd.
You save the humble,
but your eyes are on the haughty to bring them low.
You are my lamp, O LORD;
the LORD turns my darkness into light.
With your help I can advance against a troop;
with my God I can scale a wall.
As for God, his way is perfect;
the word of the LORD is flawless.
He is a shield
for all who take refuge in him.
For who is God besides the LORD?
And who is the Rock except our God?
It is God who arms me with strength
and makes my way perfect.
He makes my feet like the feet of a deer;
he enables me to stand on the heights.
He trains my hands for battle;
my arms can bend a bow of bronze.
You give me your shield of victory;
you stoop down to make me great.

2 Samuel 22:26-36

Vilhelm Hammershøi, "From the Deerpark near Copenhagen"

Psalm 5

Give ear to my words, O LORD,
consider my sighing.
Listen to my cry for help,
my King and my God,
for to you I pray.
In the morning, O LORD, you hear my voice;
in the morning I lay my requests before you
and wait in expectation.
You are not a God who takes pleasure in evil;
with you the wicked cannot dwell.
The arrogant cannot stand in your presence;
you hate all who do wrong.
You destroy those who tell lies;
bloodthirsty and deceitful men
the LORD abhors.
But I, by your great mercy,
will come into your house;
in reverence will I bow down
towards your holy temple.
Lead me, O LORD, in your righteousness
because of my enemies -
make straight your way before me.

Not a word from their mouth can be trusted;
their heart is filled with destruction.
Their throat is an open grave;
with their tongue they speak deceit.
Declare them guilty, O God!
Let their intrigues be their downfall.
Banish them for their many sins,
for they have rebelled against you.
But let all who take refuge in you be glad;
let them ever sing for joy.
Spread your protection over them,
that those who love your name may rejoice in you.
For surely, O LORD, you bless the righteous;
you surround them with your favour as with a shield.

Psalm 5:1-12

Psalm 23

The LORD is my shepherd, I shall not be in want.
He makes me lie down in green pastures,
he leads me beside quiet waters,
he restores my soul.
He guides me in paths of righteousness
for his name's sake.
Even though I walk
through the valley of the shadow of death,
I will fear no evil,
for you are with me;
your rod and your staff,
they comfort me.
You prepare a table before me
in the presence of my enemies.
You anoint my head with oil;
my cup overflows.
Surely goodness and love will follow me
all the days of my life,
and I will dwell in the house of the LORD
for ever.

Psalm 23:1-6

Paul Cezanne, "Still-life"

Psalm 116

I love the LORD, for he heard my voice;
he heard my cry for mercy.
Because he turned his ear to me,
I will call on him as long as I live.
The cords of death entangled me,
the anguish of the grave came upon me;
I was overcome by trouble and sorrow.
Then I called on the name of the LORD:
"O LORD, save me!"
The LORD is gracious and righteous;
our God is full of compassion.
The LORD protects the simple-hearted;
when I was in great need, he saved me.
Be at rest once more, O my soul,
for the LORD has been good to you.
For you, O LORD, have delivered my soul from death,
my eyes from tears,
my feet from stumbling,
that I may walk before the LORD
in the land of the living.
I believed; therefore I said,
"I am greatly afflicted."
And in my dismay I said,
"All men are liars."

How can I repay the LORD
for all his goodness to me?
I will lift up the cup of salvation
and call on the name of the LORD.
I will fulfil my vows to the LORD
in the presence of all his people.
Precious in the sight of the LORD
is the death of his saints.
O LORD, truly I am your servant;
I am your servant, the son of your maidservant;
you have freed me from my chains.
I will sacrifice a thank-offering to you
and call on the name of the LORD.
I will fulfil my vows to the LORD
in the presence of all his people,
in the courts of the house of the LORD -
in your midst, O Jerusalem.
Praise the LORD.

Psalm 116:1-19

The Song of the Vineyard

I will sing for the one I love
a song about his vineyard:
My loved one had a vineyard
on a fertile hillside.
He dug it up and cleared it of stones
and planted it with the choicest vines.
He built a watchtower in it
and cut out a winepress as well.
Then he looked for a crop of good grapes,
but it yielded only bad fruit.
"Now you dwellers in Jerusalem and men of Judah,
judge between me and my vineyard.
What more could have been done for my vineyard
than I have done for it?
When I looked for good grapes,
why did it yield only bad?
Now I will tell you
what I am going to do to my vineyard:
I will take away its hedge,
and it will be destroyed;
I will break down its wall,
and it will be trampled.
I will make it a wasteland,
neither pruned nor cultivated,
and briers and thorns will grow there.

I will command the clouds
not to rain on it."
The vineyard of the LORD Almighty
is the house of Israel,
and the men of Judah
are the garden of his delight.
And he looked for justice, but saw bloodshed;
for righteousness, but heard cries of distress.

Isaiah 5:1-7

Claude Monet, "Vase of Flowers"

Mary's Song

My soul glorifies the Lord
and my spirit rejoices in God my Saviour,
for he has been mindful
of the humble state of his servant.
From now on all generations will call me blessed,
for the Mighty One has done great things for me -
holy is his name.
His mercy extends to those who fear him,
from generation to generation.
He has performed mighty deeds with his arm;
he has scattered those who are proud in their inmost thoughts.
He has brought down rulers from their thrones
but has lifted up the humble.
He has filled the hungry with good things
but has sent the rich away empty.
He has helped his servant Israel,
remembering to be merciful
to Abraham and his descendants for ever,
even as he said to our fathers.

Luke 1:46-56

Zechariah's Song

Praise be to the Lord, the God of Israel,
because he has come and has redeemed his people.
He has raised up a horn of salvation for us
in the house of his servant David
(as he said through his holy prophets of long ago),
salvation from our enemies
and from the hand of all who hate us -
to show mercy to our fathers
and to remember his holy covenant,
the oath he swore to our father Abraham:
to rescue us from the hand of our enemies,
and to enable us to serve him without fear
in holiness and righteousness before him all our days.
And you, my child, will be called a prophet of the Most High;
for you will go on before the Lord to prepare the way for him,
to give his people the knowledge of salvation
through the forgiveness of their sins,
because of the tender mercy of our God,
by which the rising sun will come to us from heaven
to shine on those living in darkness
and in the shadow of death,
to guide our feet into the path of peace.

Luke 1:68-79

Eugene Henri Cauchoisn, "Still Life of Flowers"

Blessings and Woes

Blessed are you who are poor,
for yours is the kingdom of God.
Blessed are you who hunger now,
for you will be satisfied.
Blessed are you who weep now,
for you will laugh.
Blessed are you when men hate you,
when they exclude you and insult you
and reject your name as evil,
because of the Son of Man.
"Rejoice in that day and leap for joy,
because great is your reward in heaven.
For that is how their fathers treated the prophets.
"But woe to you who are rich,
for you have already received your comfort.
Woe to you who are well fed now,
for you will go hungry.
Woe to you who laugh now,
for you will mourn and weep.
Woe to you when all men speak well of you,
for that is how their fathers treated the false prophets.

Luke 6:20-26

The Great Multitude's
Song

All the angels were standing round the throne and around the elders and the four living creatures. They fell down on their faces before the throne and worshipped God, saying:

"Amen! Praise and glory
and wisdom and thanks and honour
and power and strength
be to our God for ever and ever.
Amen!"

Then one of the elders asked me, "These in white robes - who are they, and where did they come from?"

I answered, "Sir, you know."

And he said, "These are they who have come out of the great tribulation; they have washed their robes and made them white in the blood of the Lamb. Therefore,

"they are before the throne of God
and serve him day and night in his temple;
and he who sits on the throne will spread his tent over them.
Never again will they hunger;
never again will they thirst.
The sun will not beat upon them,
nor any scorching heat.
For the Lamb at the centre of the throne will be their shepherd;
he will lead them to springs of living water.
And God will wipe away every tear from their eyes."

Revelation 7:11-17

Picture Credits

Page 7: "Star-studded Firmament (the barrel-shaped Vault)", Mausolium of Galla Placidia, Ravenna, 425-430. Mosaic

Page 11: John Samuel Raven (1829-77), "Near Dunkeld". Roy Miles Esq. Photo: The Bridgeman Art Library

Page 14: Christian Købke, "Study of Surf near Marina Piccola, Capri", 1839. Statens Museum for Kunst, Copenhagen, Denmark. Photo: DOWIC Fotografi

Page 19: "The three Magi", Sant'Apollinare Nuovo, Ravenna, early 6th century. Mosaic

Page 21: Edouard Manet, "Moonlight on Boulogne Harbour", 1869. Musse d'Orsay, Paris, France. Photo: The Bridgeman Art Library / Peter Willi

Page 27: Vincent van Gogh, "Irises", 1889. J. Paul Getty Museum, Malibu, CA, USA. Photo: The Bridgeman Art Library

Page 31: "St. Peter and St. Andrew leave the Nets to follow Christ", Sant'Apollinare Nuovo, Ravenna, early 6th century. Mosaic

Page 35: Fedor Mikhailovich Matveev, "The Imatra Waterfall in Finland", 1819. State Russian Museum, St. Petersburg, Russia. Photo: The Bridgeman Art Library

Page 38: Madeleine Lemaire (1845-1928), "Roses". Mallett & Son Antiques Ltd., London, Uk. Photo: The Bridgeman Art Library

Page: 43: "The Paralytic left down through the Roof", Sant'Apollinare Nuovo, Ravenna, early 6th century. Mosaic

Page 46: James Abbott McNeill Whistler, "Nocturne, Blue and Silver: Battersea Reach", c. 1872/78. Isabella Stewart Gardner Museum, Boston, Massachusetts, USA. Photo: The Bridgeman Art Library

Page 51: L.A. Ring, "Thaw", 1901. Statens Museum for Kunst, Copenhagen, Denmark. Photo: DOWIC Fotografi

Page 55: "The Healing of the Madman", Sant'Apollinare Nuovo, Ravenna, early 6th century. Mosaic

Page 59: Pierre Auguste Renoir (1841-1919), "Tulips in a Vase". Noortman, Maastricht, Netherlands. Photo: The Bridgeman Art Library

Page 62: Claude Monet, "Poplars on the Epte", c. 1891, National Gallery of Scotland, Edinburgh, Scotland. Photo: The Bridgeman Art Library

Page 67: "The Samaritan Woman at the Well", Sant'Apollinare Nuovo, Ravenna, early 6th century. Mosaic

Page 70: Adelsteen Normann (1848-1918), "A Fjord Steamer". Bonhams, London, UK. Photo: The Bridgeman Art Library

Page 75: Maurice Galbraith Cullen, "On the St. Lawrence", 1897. Art Gallery of Ontario, Toronto, Canada. Photo: The Bridgeman Art Library

Page 79:"Noah releasing the white Dove", San Marco, Venice, Italy. Mosaic

Page 83: William Turner, "Moonlight over the Lake of Lucerne from the Rigi, in the distance", 1841/42. Whitworth Art Gallery, Manchester, UK.

Photo: AKG Berlin

Page 87: Vilhelm Hammershøi, "Dust Motes dancing in Sunlight", 1900.

Ordrupgaard, Copenhagen, Denmark. Photo: Ole Woldbye

Page 91: "Christ separates the Sheep fom the Goats", Sant'Apollinare Nuovo, Ravenna, early 6th century. Mosaic

Page 94: Johannes Martin Grimelund (1842-1917), "Summer Morning at Molde". Musee Crozatier, Le Puy-en-Velay, France. Photo: The Bridgeman Art Library

Page 99: W. Weiss (fl.c.1840), "Still life with strawberries". Roy Miles Esq. Photo: The Bridgeman Art Library

Page 103: "Detail of the Greek Fret", Mausolium of Galla Placidia, Ravenna, early 5th century. Mosaic

Page 106: Fritz Syberg, "Overkærby Hill. Winter", 1917. Statens Museum for Kunst, Copenhagen, Denmark. Photo: DOWIC Fotografi

Page 111: Vilhelm Hammershøi, "From the Deerpark near Copenhagen", 1901. Statens Museum for Kunst, Copenhagen, Denmark. Photo: DOWIC Fotografi

Page 115: Paul Cezanne, "Still-life", 1888/90. Musee d'Orsay, Paris, France. Photo: AKG Berlin

Page 119: Anna Syberg: "Roses", 1902. Faaborg Museum, Denmark. Photo: Faaborg Museum

Page 120: Claude Monet, "Vase of Flowers", c. 1881/82. Courtauld Gallery, London, UK. Photo: The Bridgeman Art Library

Page 123: Caspar David Friedrich, "Before Sunrise", 1830/34. National Gallerie, SMPK, Berlin, Germany. Photo: AKG Berlin

Page 124: Eugene Henri Cauchoisn (1850-1911), "Still Life of Flowers". Private Collection, Gavin Graham Gallery. Photo: The Bridgeman Art Library

Page 127:Isaak Ilyich Levitan (1860-1900), "Above Eternal Repose". Tretyakov Gallery, Moscow, Russia. Photo: The Bridgeman Art Library